Praise for T

The Token is accessible and practical—ideal for everyone working in groups, schools, workplaces, and other projects and organizations where diversity and equity are the goals. Farmer has done an excellent job of laying out the case for, and path towards, building an inclusive organization. An excellent resource for all those who are committed to equity and need ideas and suggestions, exercises, and guidelines for moving your organization to the next level.

— Paul Kivel, educator, activist, author, *Uprooting Racism:
How White People Can Work for Racial Justice*

The Token manages to be both blunt and nuanced in a way that feels helpful and honest. Crystal Byrd Farmer does an excellent job of bringing forth really clear "dos" and "don'ts" while also acknowledging and exploring the complexity and evolving nature of the work that's required to create inclusive and equitable organizations.

— Tomis Parker, co-founder, Agile Learning Centers Network,
board member, The Alliance for Self-Directed Education

In an honest and unfiltered voice, Crystal Byrd Farmer's book provides essential guidance for white groups interested in racial equity, diversity, and inclusion. The book is a treasure trove of tools, stories, and resources for working on racism and white supremacy culture in majority white groups—especially those who consider themselves progressive or alternative. For us white folks, Crystal Byrd Farmer's experiences and no-nonsense perspective are much-needed gifts. Her book challenges us to listen, reflect, and work harder to overcome the racism in ourselves and in our communities.

— Joe Cole, Ph.D., Academic Professional Assistant Professor,
University of North Carolina, Department of Peace
and Conflict Studies, facilitator

This is the book that is going to save you from theory and guilt trips disguised as training or solutions to issues of equity and diversity. Crystal has brilliantly highlighted her personal experiences as means of examining and learning how biases affect some Black women in particular, and many intentional communities across age and gender, among other differences. She then brings in the history and pattern of anti-Black racism in particular, and offers resources and conversation prompts to work through what she brings up in these pages. I found this book refreshing in its departure from scholarly research over real-life experiences, feelings that words often fail, and so much more in terms of nuance and layers. I loved this and I'm grateful to Crystal for adding her perspectives to the conversation about relationships and diversity without apology, and with no problem being dynamic and human in her approach. Read this book!

— Akilah S. Richards, author,
Raising Free People: Unschooling
and *Liberation* and *Healing Work*

If you want to transition your organization or community to become more accessible for marginalized people, you should read this book—ideally read it first! Filled with real talk and practical exercises, *The Token* is an essential guide for how to do The Work. Not sure what The Work is? Don't worry, your new Black friend, Crystal Farmer, is here to help.

— Cynthia Tina, Co-Director,
Foundation for Intentional Community

As a co-organizer of a mostly white community focused on personal/interpersonal healing and social change, I was delighted to receive this brief gem of a book by Crystal Byrd Farmer. In her blunt, no-nonsense authorial voice, Farmer gave me exactly the information and the step-by-step plans my team needs to move forward with our community's anti-racism work. Farmer's advice on how to honor and protect a group's "tokens" is a powerful and innovative teaching that we have already put to good use. I wish this book had been available for navigating challenges in recent years.

— Sarah Taub, Center for a New Culture

The Token

THE TOKEN

Common Sense Ideas for
Increasing Diversity in Your Organization

Crystal Byrd Farmer

new society
PUBLISHERS

Cover design by Diane McIntosh.

Printed in Canada. First printing September, 2020

Inquiries regarding requests to reprint all or part of *The Token* should be addressed to New Society Publishers at the address below. To order directly from the publishers, please call toll-free (North America) 1-800-567-6772, or order online at www.newsociety.com

Any other inquiries can be directed by mail to:

New Society Publishers
P.O. Box 189, Gabriola Island, BC V0R 1X0, Canada
(250) 247-9737

LIBRARY AND ARCHIVES CANADA CATALOGUING IN PUBLICATION

Title: The token : common sense ideas for increasing diversity in your organization / Crystal Byrd Farmer.

Names: Farmer, Crystal Byrd, 1985– author.

Description: Includes index.

Identifiers: Canadiana (print) 20200251597 |
Canadiana (ebook) 20200251651 |
ISBN 9780865719514 (softcover) | ISBN 9781550927443 (PDF) |
ISBN 9781771423403 (EPUB)

Subjects: LCSH: Diversity in the workplace. |
LCSH: Personnel management.

Classification: LCC HF5549.5.M5 F37 2020 | DDC 658.30089—dc23

Funded by the Government of Canada   Financé par le gouvernement du Canada

New Society Publishers' mission is to publish books that contribute in fundamental ways to building an ecologically sustainable and just society, and to do so with the least possible impact on the environment, in a manner that models this vision.

To all my teachers,
whether they intended to be one or not

Contents

Preface

It started with composting toilets. In 2016, Foundation for Intentional Community Executive Director Sky Blue invited me to speak at the Twin Oaks Communities Conference in rural Virginia. I had been involved in the intentional communities movement for a few years, but Twin Oaks was the first commune I had ever visited. While I was lucky to stay in a fully-plumbed cabin during the weekend, the conference site only had composting toilets for attendees. The joy that what I call hippy-dippy people have about suffering for the sake of the environment constantly amazes me. The only thing I could think about was my grandmother, who grew up without indoor plumbing. The overwhelming thought I had was, "Black people would not put up with this."

After the conference, I wrote an article for *Communities* magazine explaining how people of color could feel left out in intentional communities. A year later, I was honored to be on a panel with other Black and brown communitarians who discussed their experiences with white progressives who thought they were doing their best. I have never lived officially "in community," but I was already picking up on the big problem: they want us, but they don't want *us*. That's when I understood that people who believe they're doing the work of anti-oppression are just barely scratching the surface. So I wrote this book. Nothing in it is revolutionary. There are plenty of blogs and diversity trainings that can help you understand what it means to be marginalized, but there's only one me. I'm going to tell it my way, and I hope you find it helpful.

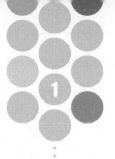

I'm Your New Black Friend

Hi, I'm Crystal. I'm a Token, which means I often show up in communities as the only Black person. I'm not just Black: I'm a woman, bisexual, autistic, and disabled, and sometimes I'm the only one in all of those categories. When we talk about wanting diversity in an organization, we mean we want people who have different types of identity. That's hard to do, because while our differences make us special, our similarities make us comfortable.

You like being comfortable. You are part of a community or workplace, and you probably have a majority of certain identities in your membership. In the US and Western Europe, most organizations are majority white, educated, and middle-class. When you are in the majority, you make the rules, which means moving through the world is easier for you. When someone who is not in the majority tries to move through the same world, they may have difficulty. That's why those people are called marginalized. They live their lives in the asterisks and footnotes of majority culture. I'm here to explain what the marginalized people in your community experience, and how you can make your organization more comfortable for them.

Whether you are organizing vegans, moms, or local history buffs, you probably want diversity. You heard somewhere that diversity is great, and you've tried to recruit people who don't look like you. You're really passionate about your community, but you're confused why people from [insert marginalized group here] never come out or apply. That's why I'm here. I've spent all of my life in community. From engineers to kinksters, Methodists to polyamorists, I've been a Token in many different situations. At some point I accepted the Crown of Tokenism and ran with it. I've spent my time trying to increase diversity in different organizations as well as speaking and writing about it. I'm usually the bearer of bad news, because diversity is less about the people you're attracting than it is about you—your values, your culture, and your community.

Here are three steps towards making your organization more diverse:

1. Prepare your community
2. Do The Work
3. Create culture conscious spaces

In order to transform into an organization that is more comfortable to marginalized people, you must do what I call The Work. The Work is called anti-racism or anti-oppression work because you are undoing power imbalances to lift up the marginalized voices in your community. I describe how to get prepared for The Work in the first part of this book. In the second part, I talk about the basics of privilege, bias, and microaggressions. Each section ends with discussion questions to help your members start doing The Work. Finally, I give practical ways that you can create meeting spaces that are more comfortable for everyone.

You may wonder, "Why should I change our community in the name of diversity? Our community is great, and great people will be attracted to it!" The truth is that access is a privilege. If you are privileged, you don't naturally see the obstacles marginalized people face in their everyday lives. You may have heard things about Black people getting stopped by police more often or being followed around stores. Whether you believe those things happen or not, ethnic minorities have a different experience of the world. It's a similar story for queer people, people with disabilities, religious minorities, and immigrants. Lack of access is not just in our heads—it has been researched and documented by scholars and YouTubers. The stress from lack of access makes showing up in a community difficult. We have to spend energy coping with implicit bias and microaggressions. When we use all of our energy, we have less energy to do the things we want to do. We might only show a part of ourselves, or we might not show up at all.

You may think, "I already know this! I'm a great ally!" Stay tuned. Even people who think they are helping are sometimes causing harm. I find this to be true when we cross categories of marginalization (sometimes called intersectionality). For instance, you may be white and identify as queer, which leads you to feel empathy for Black people because you have been denied some civil rights. The truth is there could be ways you are alienating your Black members even with some shared experiences. I wrote this book for you, too.

If you are a Token, God bless you. The work you are doing will be thankless and hard. This book will help you to talk to your community's leadership so you don't tear your hair out. Before you start, I want you to build layers of support inside

> I understand Token is a negative term. In the context of this book, I'm using it to identify the people in your organization who may feel left out because of their identity. I don't recommend calling them Tokens to their faces, but you should ask for their input during this process.

and outside your community. Use your self-care tools, and know that it is OK to take a break or stop the work completely. No work in community is worth your peace of mind.

There's a saying in the autistic community: If you've met one person with autism, you've met one person with autism. When you finish this book, you'll have met one Black, queer, autistic woman with opinions. While I hope my experiences translate across space and time, I don't assume they will always fit your situation. Test my theories on your marginalized friends (with consent). If you don't have any, start paying people to educate you. If you're going to be a good leader, you need people who can be honest with you while sparing your feelings.

More on terminology: Why is Black capitalized? A friend started doing it on social media, and I liked it. Black is an identity, not just a social construct. Many white people don't believe they are white, so they don't get a capital letter. Why use the word queer? It's easier than spelling LGBTQ+, but that's exactly the community I'm referring to. What about disabled vs person with disability? I don't have a preference, but people say they prefer person with disability, unless they're autistic. If you've already started writing me a letter about all that, keep your pen handy.

Why aren't you using the terms people of color (POC) or Black, Indigenous, and people of color (BIPOC)? I am Black and not a representative of other people of color, which could include Latinx or Hispanic, Asian, African, Indigenous, and everyone else who does not pass as white on a regular basis. While I am sure that my tips are relevant and useful to all those groups, I can only speak with authority on those identities I am familiar with.

Furthermore, there is an eagerness on the side of progressives to lump Black people in with other POCs. While many countries experienced the dark legacy of colonization, people of the African diaspora are a unique case. The things that will create an inclusive environment for Black people are not always the same for other people of color. In this book, I encourage you to think about how to include Black people in your community instead of congratulating yourself because you have some people of color. Other marginalized people—especially the ones in your community—can help you understand the challenges unique to them.

Finally, I am always learning, but I'm a little stubborn. I grew up in a time where bisexuality meant attraction to two genders and transgender was a one-way ticket. Now, people refer to multiple genders and a nonbinary spectrum. Language and culture change, and I try to use words that are acceptable in the current time. There may be a point where this book is both outdated and problematic. Call me out or call me in, but I fully believe that problematic writing can be used for good. If my language doesn't work for you, write your own book.

Preparing for Change

When I worked in corporate America, I felt like I was judged more harshly than my peers. I was an engineer, so not only was I often the only Black person on my team, I was usually the only woman. When I disagreed with my boss, I was accused of being insubordinate. When I took sick days to care for my daughter, I was assumed to be slacking. When I didn't waste time gossiping, I was told I was not a team player. Many well-intentioned HR managers have welcomed marginalized people with the vision of a diverse organization, but they don't actually want diversity. They want the appearance of diversity while everyone conforms to white middle-class culture. In my job interviews, I used to ask, "What is the diversity like?" The most revealing answer was from a female Asian engineer, who immediately said, "We don't have a problem with diversity." Community organizations often react the same way.

When I talk about doing The Work, I mean the process of examining your internal beliefs about your world and the marginalized people you encounter. You have to learn what your biases are in order to counteract them. You have to understand your culture to help others adapt to it. You have to acknowledge your privilege to counterbalance it. If you are able to see the way your life differs from the lives of marginalized people, you are more able to help them feel more welcome and included.

The simple act of asking, "Is our community diverse?" will spark both movement and resistance in members of your organization. Prepare to engage with personal conversations, group discussions, and, if necessary, outside facilitators. You need to know who will help and who will hurt your efforts. The next two chapters talk about your team members and the resistance—people who will oppose you along the way. If you already feel overwhelmed, consider hiring a diversity consultant or facilitator. This is only the first wave. Once you start making changes, you will have even stronger responses to integrate and resolve.

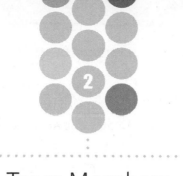

Team Members

Don't do The Work alone. When you are trying to enact change in your community, it helps to have different types of people on your team.

Cocreators

Talk to your leadership about your desire for diversity. Try to get the majority of them on board before starting The Work. This may mean intense conversations about why it's important and what your vision is. Your cocreators don't need to be "woke" or experts on marginalization, but they should be open to the idea of improving the organization. Ideally, you want people with different strengths on your team: someone who can inspire people by painting a vision, someone who can talk extemporaneously about goals, someone who can respond to emails from concerned members, and someone who can facilitate conflict in the moment. If only one person fits all of those, send the rest to leadership development. If you have leaders with different years of experience, make sure that you have a mix of Young Turks and old hats in agreement. A united leadership is key to making changes more palatable to the community. If members identify warring cohorts in leadership, they will start thinking in terms of "us" versus "them," and your efforts will be less effective.

Tokens

Identify the people who are "one of the only ones," and talk to them about your plans. Don't engage them so they can educate you or encourage you. If you would ask me, I'd say it's too hard and you're going to fail. What you want to do is tell your Tokens that you will be talking more about diversity in your community, you anticipate some changes in policies, and you will shield them from the worst of your community members' reactions. If your Tokens are in leadership positions, discuss the same considerations and ensure that they have a support system of people that identify as they do.

Cheerleaders

It's helpful to involve people outside your community who know you well. These are people you can vent to and get advice from, but they don't have decision-making power in your organization. You should have a close relationship with these people before you start. Do not choose a marginalized person just because they are in the category you want to target. Leaders tend to depend on marginalized people to carry the emotional load for them while doing The Work. They see such

> My favorite type of interaction is when privileged people come up to me and tell me how grateful they are for what I'm doing. I'm shining a light on the dark world of oppression. The reality is that most groups never get The Work done. They leave diversity training feeling like they are the good guys, but they usually don't do what I've asked them to do and make systemic change. I'm shining a light, but all too often you're taking the flashlight and turning it off.

marginalized people not as experts in their chosen field, but as experts about their category of marginalization. If you are reaching out to a marginalized person to tell them about the hard work you've been doing around anti-oppression, stop. That person should be compensated for doing your Work.

The Resistance

You will encounter resistance from your community members when you start doing The Work. That's because while most people are OK with the idea of diversity, they are usually not willing to experience discomfort for the sake of it. People join communities for various reasons. They may not see the connection between diversity and getting more out of their community. As a leader, you have to make the case for diversity. You also have to shepherd your group through the process of doing The Work. This is not something you can cover in an afternoon workshop. Explain the changes, make them, and explain them again. Talk with every single member who has concerns. Endure the drama. You may have people leave. You may have a splinter group trying to undermine you. You will have immense pressure to change your plans and go back to the way things were. Keep your vision in mind, and don't stop just because it's hard.

Before you start putting out fires, build trusting relationships between the leadership and your Tokens. They will inevitably be the target of backlash, especially if they have been vocal about the changes. Do not wait for your Tokens to come to you to set up a plan. If your organization has handled conflict badly in the past, take the time to learn mediation skills. Restorative or transformative justice are both models that progressive organizations have used to address harm done by people in community. Whatever you do, be transparent about your conflict resolution steps.

Why This? Why Now?

There are resistors who think pointing out our differences causes divisiveness. These people may think that if we only focused on what we have in common, our lives would be better. Marginalized people are marginalized because the majority culture sees our differences as a problem. Ignoring those differences means ignoring part of our identity. Tell your members that minimizing the difficulties your Tokens face harms them.

When you start talking about increasing diversity, resistors may bring up other problems in the organization. They may claim that other problems should be solved first because they are more important. If you are focusing on race, they may insist on disability access or LGBTQ+ inclusion. Think through and document why you're focusing on some aspects and not others. It's not fair to tell a marginalized group that they are less important, but there are limits to your community's energy. The resistor may have a legitimate concern that could be addressed in the future.

Some resistors who have any of the privileged identities may start complaining that they are being targeted. Resistors may believe that you plan on implementing extreme policies such as limiting the number of white members or starting all meetings with an apology to marginalized people. They may take up space by bringing up examples of so-called reverse discrimination or explaining what their closest Black relative believes. They may spend time wallowing in guilt and begging for forgiveness. If they are not speaking about it in meetings, they may be talking about it to other community members in private or on social media.

When you begin to talk about marginalization, many people fear that creating equity will put them at a disadvantage. They may have never considered that most of their success in life is based on identity and not their own skills and talent. They don't want something "taken from them" and "given away," as if equity were cupcakes at a birthday party. This part of The Work is important, but it has to be done away from your Tokens. Give your privileged members their own time and space to process their feelings, and ask trusted members to be their listening ear. It may just take one personal conversation to help the resistor understand that what they are doing may harm others.

If the resistance continues, take action. Agree in advance on how to deal with personal attacks and disparaging comments. Ask your Tokens if they need help blocking the members on social media. Assign a leader or member to be their backup, arguing for them against the resistor. Use your conflict resolution steps to censure the resistor and remove them if they are not willing to be respectful. You may lose more than that resistor even when you have a fair and transparent process, but it's important to follow through.

The Willfully Blind

Many people will simply not believe that marginalized people need accommodations. Research shows that many white people believe Black people have achieved all their goals of racial justice in the US. The Fair Housing Act of 1968 made discrimination based on race illegal, but Black families in the 21st century consistently have a harder time getting mortgages than white families. The one Black family you see in your neighborhood is just a small slice of the families that may have had the same income but were unable to obtain a mortgage and financing.

Many people who seek to build communities in majority white areas believe that Black people are less educated, less able to keep and maintain wealth, and more prone to crime and drug use. These assumptions are not inherent to Blackness or any minority. Doing The Work means letting go of assumptions about wealth and quality of character. Changing standards to let more people participate is not actually lowering standards; it is recognizing the impact of systemic discrimination.

People choose to be in community because they share something in common. Some resistors have assumptions about a minority's culture that gives them the impression that they are not a good fit for the community. I was once interviewed by a Black parent about the Agile Learning Center I co-founded, Gastonia Freedom School. She asked if we were welcoming to LGBTQ+ people, and I said that we were. She spent a few minutes talking about what she had learned now that she was around more of them, and how she respected their struggle even though her religion was against homosexuality.

I did not tell her I was queer or that she was a bad person, but I did say that it was important to form personal relationships with people to understand the difficulties they may face. That's what we want our children to do, and that's what she was doing. Your community may be afraid that some cultures are more racist, sexist, or homophobic than the majority culture, but the reality is that there are all types of people in all places. Be willing to have a conversation about your shared values and ideals to help others understand who would be a good fit regardless of their assumed culture.

On a different point, there are marginalized people who have not experienced systemic discrimination or who do not attribute any setbacks in their lives to their identity. Their lived experience is just as valid as anyone else's, but do not use one Token's experience to argue against another's. Believe both of them. Understand that systemic patterns are not always applicable to individual experiences. If a Token is happy with the way their life has gone, celebrate. Just don't believe that one positive experience means all oppression has been solved.

Finally, some people who are unwilling to engage with racism may fear that accepting racism as a fact diminishes the view of the USA as the land of opportunity and freedom. The founding fathers believed whiteness and wealth gave them moral superiority. The subjugation of minorities was designed purposefully and embedded in our founding documents. Changing that system means fighting the very character of our country. It feels bad. It feels painful. It feels necessary.

My Time to Shine

There will be people in your organization who are initially interested in helping increase diversity. They may be positive and encouraging as long as they have control over the direction and outcome. This resistor may be a person in leadership or someone who wants to get the credit for increasing diversity in the organization. This person may even be a Token. As other resistors pop up, however, they may become discouraged. They may think The Work is not worth the conflict and stress. They may start asking to focus on other issues or to take a break so that emotions can die down. Conflict is not what kills communities, but the inability to handle it is. Embrace conflict but don't alienate people. Before you continue The Work, renew your commitment to diversity and to the community itself. If your leadership cannot continue without infighting, hire a facilitator.

Your Tokens are people too, which means sometimes they can be assholes. Part of your job as a leader is to help people feel included without endorsing harmful behavior. Marginalized people may have legitimate trauma from harms related to their identity. Unless you are a support group, your community is not the place for Tokens to heal. Tokens are just as responsible for doing their work while you are doing The Work. Use your conflict resolution tools to avoid dramatic moments where the Token declares, "You just hate me because I'm Black!"

The word ally has come to mean someone who is not part of a marginalized population but supports them. I think many people are quick to call themselves allies without doing The Work. You may be surprised when marginalized people criticize actions that you see as good and necessary. That is because privileged, white liberals have always positioned themselves above race. They ignore issues important to minorities in order to avoid being divisive and achieve their goals. That's why white women received the right to vote decades before Black women— they were willing to work within the white supremacist system because it benefited them even as it harmed others.

It is vital that your work include interacting with other privileged people instead of proving how much of an ally you are to marginalized people. Don't expect praise from marginalized people when you talk about the work you are doing. You are fulfilling your responsibility to community, not auditioning for Volunteer of the Month. Better yet, don't talk to marginalized people about the work you are doing at all. Ask them about their struggles and victories, and just listen without giving advice or adding your own stories.

Doing The Work

Use the following chapters to help your community do The Work. In each section, I explain a key part of how marginalization works, followed by discussion questions for your members. You may need to adapt these questions to your particular setting. I recommend doing the discussions over several weeks instead of piling them into one day. The Work is an ongoing process, and your members need time to see how oppression shows up in their daily lives. When it is time to get feedback from your Tokens, your community may need several weeks of processing to understand that a negative event occurred not because someone is a bad person, but because they didn't recognize how they caused harm even with the best intentions.

Diversity Training

You can present the major ideas of The Work in various ways. You can talk through the principles I have laid out using the suggested resources. You can hire consultants to lead diversity training. You can show films or have guest speakers talk about their experiences with marginalization. The form of the training is not as important as the conversations that follow. Do not ask your Tokens to lead your training or share their experiences in an unmoderated forum. With strangers, community members can ask impersonal questions and argue with people who have experience dealing with doubters. If your Tokens have to spend their energy defending their identity, they may not feel safe sharing their thoughts on other subjects.

Unless they are in leadership, give your Tokens the choice to opt out of diversity training. I have experienced well-meaning facilitators who get to a point where they want people to announce ways that they have less or more privilege. When I'm the only Black person in the room, I feel immense pressure to state that I'm Black and I know I have less privilege. That is, in fact, the point of the exercise. But it does me no good to identify myself as a minority.

Good diversity training is about people with privilege reconciling that privilege with their view of the world as just, fair, and equal. If I could, I would have every white person stand up and say, "I am white, and I have privilege." That's tough to do. You know you are a good person, and you have never intentionally discriminated against someone. You want to avoid talking about your privilege and instead focus on being sorry for those who don't have it. That is not The Work.

People will need space to process their feelings. They will struggle with the idea that privilege means they have an easier life. They will come up with times they've had difficulty because of their identity. They will argue that they know several marginalized people who like them just the way they are. They will remember the things they or their relatives have done that were racist, sexist, or homophobic. This is all good to do. But, as a Token, I don't need or want to hear that. It's tiring to bear the emotional burden of empathizing with and forgiving every privileged person. I'd rather meet you on the other side, when you've accepted your privilege and are ready to act in ways that benefit both of us.

> When I pointed out a microaggression in a group, someone asked why I always had to make it about race. Most white people live with the delusion that race doesn't affect their lives. Unlike them, I see the race of the people I'm interacting with. I change my actions when I know my identity matters. When something bad happens, I have to consider how race colors the outcome. My expectations for customer service, my well-being, and my life depend on me making sure these interactions go well. When I describe a negative experience, I'm not trying to shame the people around me. I'm educating them. If they feel guilty about it, that's their Work to do.

I repeat: subjecting your Token to your sob story about being white and ignorant is not part of The Work. If you are making a marginalized person listen to you process your emotions, you should be paying them. Even if you are covering multiple categories of marginalization, your Token is probably more adept at navigating their privilege than you are. Host a separate discussion or training for them if you have the resources.

Community Feedback

The Work requires active participation from your community members. Seek to understand your privileged members' views on diversity before you try to change them. For instance, many people assume that people from different backgrounds don't come because they don't do whatever your community does. There are stereotypes about Black people not swimming, camping, or drinking craft beer. I know people who do all of those. Before you count a minority group out, search online for that group and your activity. There are marginalized people who are looking for what you're offering. They are waiting for you to show that you are inclusive and ready to accept them. If your members do see a need for more diversity, avoid setting unrealistic goals. It's unrealistic to expect a gathering in a majority white area to be 40% Black, but it could definitely happen in a place with a larger Black population. If you're going to set a numeric goal (and I suggest you don't), strive to make your membership proportional to the demographics in your area.

Asking for feedback from your Tokens is another key step. Take time to understand their personal journeys and how they feel about being a part of your community. Always ask for consent first. Instead of saying, "Are you OK being the only Asian in our group?" Say, "I was wondering if I could ask about your experience as a person of color." Your Tokens do not owe you any feedback ever. In fact, appreciate them for taking the time to show up. If they are willing to give feedback, it's a bonus. Listen to your Tokens' feedback with an open mind, and do not comment on the feasibility of their suggestions yet. Undoubtedly, you will hear stories from your Tokens that are either painful and/or alarming. Do not rush to take care of the individual harm done unless it involves safety concerns. See the harms as part of a larger pattern, and commit to fixing the issue at the root and not on the surface.

In one two-week period I was pulled over by police four times. Prior to that, I had only been pulled over twice in my life. I was traveling long distances to work, and instead of my old Honda, I was driving a rental muscle car. Research shows that police officers stop Black drivers disproportionately across the US and Canada. More stops means more opportunities for a ticket, for arrest, and for a fatal shooting. When I talk about being pulled over, I don't expect the listener to go to the police station and demand to talk to the chief. I would rather they acknowledge that there is a systemic problem in the way police do their work. I want them to challenge the police to address their bias and ask the government to provide relief to people who have been harmed by over-policing. When marginalized people tell their stories, we are asking for systemic change and not just a bandage. Don't rush to fix problems in your community without digging to the root cause.

You will get negative feedback no matter what type of community you have. What you do with the feedback is your prerogative. If you care about diversity (and you're reading this book, after all) listen closely to feedback from your minority participants. It's not that their feedback is more important, but, as the Tokens, they may be speaking to things that you are not aware of. Some of the feedback may hit a nerve. Do not respond by telling your Tokens that they are too sensitive and that your group is really trying. If you're progressive, we hope you're trying. That doesn't mean you're succeeding.

Identity:

My Privilege Is Better Than Yours

There are multiple categories of identity, and for each category, there are people who have less privilege and people who have more. To have less privilege means that some things, like getting a job, may be harder for them than a person with more privilege. For instance, there are plenty of Black people in upper level management positions, but on average white people get promoted more often than their Black counterparts. Privilege doesn't count on individual strengths—privilege is all about someone's identity.

Having less privilege also means that you may have more harmful assumptions made about you than a person with more privilege. For instance, immigrants are often seen as less educated regardless of their education level in their native country. You may know these assumptions are wrong, but implicit bias means that you are assuming it before you are even aware of it (more about that later).

Use the following chart to help your members identify where they may or may not have privilege.

These categories are very broad and vary based on your community. In fact, people who identify in similar ways may

Figure 1

Category	More Privilege	Less Privilege
Race*	White	Black, Asian, Indigenous, etc.
Ethnicity**	European Descent	African Descent, Asian, Hispanic, etc.
Socioeconomic Status	Wealthy, Middle Class	Low Income
Gender	Male	Female, Nonbinary, Transgender, Intersex
Sexual Orientation	Straight, Bisexual	Gay, Lesbian, Pansexual, etc.
National Origin***	North American, European	South American, Middle Eastern, African, Southeast Asian, etc.
First Language	English	Spanish, Chinese, etc.
Disability Status	Able-Bodied	Disabled
Age	Older	Younger
Education	Bachelors, Masters, Doctorate	High School Diploma, Associates, Certificate
Religion	Christian, Jewish	Muslim, Hindu, etc.
Immigration Status	Native	Immigrant, Aboriginal or Indigenous

* Race is defined by skin color combined with ethnic ancestry. For instance, a person can be from the US, Brazil, or Ethiopia and identify as Black because they have African ancestry. The term African-American is used interchangeably with Black in the US.

** Ethnicity is defined by ancestral country of origin. For instance, descendants of immigrants to the US could identify as Nigerian, Cuban, or Russian. Descendants of enslaved Africans usually identify as Black when they aren't aware of specific countries of origin. Jewish can be considered an ethnicity that doesn't depend on country of origin, but parentage and religion.

*** National origin is a person's birth country.

have different experiences depending on who is in the majority around them. There is also the ability to "pass" or be perceived as part of one group while actually being in another. This means that marginalization is not one size fits all. When seeking to increase diversity, try to apply solutions that are specific to one targeted demographic instead of trying to include everyone all at once.

When starting The Work, many people refuse to see themselves as part of a majority group. They may not feel white because they've never associated themselves with whiteness. They may believe that since everyone usually acts with the best intentions, minorities are nearly always treated as equal. This is where The Work is vital. Race is a social construct enforced by society and legislation. In fact, whiteness as a concept was created at the same time that Europeans switched from using other white people as slaves to using Africans. Even after the abolition of slavery and independence movements across the world, whiteness is still considered neutral and good while other races are the Other. Think about the last time a white person was arrested for hanging out in a coffee shop. Being white doesn't mean you are personally responsible for harms other white people commit, but it does mean that you have a responsibility to address privilege when you see it causing harm.

Once they place themselves into categories, your community members have to acknowledge their privilege. Some people will bend over backwards claiming that they have not had an easier life and that they struggle too. It can be true that someone has privilege and that their life has been hard. Privilege doesn't mean the absence of difficulty; it only means that a different group has additional difficulties. There are plenty of marginalized people leading successful lives, and hopefully they are an example of what happens when people are treated equitably. When race comes up, many people will claim they are a mix of races and that their ancestors (usually Irish) may have been enslaved. It is OK to hold that truth while acknowledging that whiteness is associated with privilege. If you pass as white, you are reaping the benefits of being white. If you don't know if you pass as white, ask a Black person.

Finally, there are many other types of diversity in the world: early birds versus night owls, introverts versus extroverts, Coke drinkers versus Pepsi lovers. While these categories of diversity may be useful for building connections between your members, they are not areas where people usually experience marginalization. Do not get distracted from The Work by making your diversity tent too big. If there is Work to do, it is usually about race. If you believe your race issues are solved, have your Token write you a certificate of achievement and move on to the next category.

While classifying myself for a book seems reductionist, I think it's important to detail who I am so you understand some of my experiences in community. While I may interact more often with white progressives than others choose to, my experiences will ring true for many minorities. I use examples from my life not to shame people, but to explain how people can do better. I'm not an angry Black woman; I'm just here to tell the truth, which is neither nice nor redeeming. If you need either of those to be an effective ally to marginalized people, you're doing it wrong.

My Identities

Black. Both of my parents are descended from slaves who lived in South Carolina. There is at least one white ancestor on my mother's side, giving several of my family members a "high yella" or light-skinned complexion. None of them passed or lived as white as far as I know. While I've never questioned my Blackness, I have had trouble fitting in with my family and majority Black neighborhood. My autistic mind never quite understood cultural traditions like "playing the dozens," where friends trade off making fun of each other. Now that I'm older, I fit into the category of "blerds," Black nerds who embrace their geekiness along with their Blackness.

Cisgender Woman. Like many people, I never questioned my gender growing up. I wore skirts in middle school, but I was also drawn to so-called masculine hobbies like science experiments and model race cars. I studied mechanical engineering in college and enjoyed being the Token girl. I led our Society of Women Engineers chapter and figured out that I didn't even fit in with female engineers. I have a rational, emotionless brain that avoids drama, so I gravitated toward my white male colleagues who kept conflict to a minimum. I left the engineering field after eight years and spent some time working at public schools. Moving to a majority female working environment was eye-opening for me. No one questioned my competence, and everyone wanted to help me succeed. Even though I still had differences, I no longer felt like a Token.

Autistic. Speaking of a rational, emotionless brain, I have a diagnosis of autism. More and more children and adults are being diagnosed due to a change in the diagnostic criteria. Medical professionals now understand that autism presents differently in different genders. Starting at a young age, girls have a tendency to mask their symptoms to fit in better with neurotypical culture. Many women receive diagnoses of depression, anxiety, bipolar disorder, or other mental health issues instead of receiving help for their underlying communication and sensory issues. One of my biggest deficits is in communication. I'd like to say I'm a pretty good writer and speaker, but I'm blunt to the point of rudeness. People often attach emotions or intent to my words when I'm simply stating facts. I have learned to have relationships with people who can tolerate my black and white thinking and adjust their own wording.

Christian. In the US South, the majority of people grow up going to some kind of church. I identified strongly with Christianity through college, where I became part of progressive Christian culture (the people responsible for Beers and Hymns). Being one of the only ones who questioned evangelical Christianity caused me to be skeptical of other believers, especially when they say they love and welcome all people. Now I am a Unitarian Universalist, and I think many of their congregations support The Work, but they don't have a large enough population of marginalized people to hold them accountable.

Educated. In my school system, Black and poor students were placed into minimum requirement classes where they spent more time on discipline than school work. They Tokenized a few of us by placing us in the academically gifted classes. Though both of my parents and some of my aunts attended college, my cousins and I were the first to attend four-year universities. Working as an engineer meant my social circle included highly educated people who often had no idea of the difficulties faced by less educated people.

Lower Income. I grew up in what is still called the ghetto or hood. I went to a majority Black elementary school where 99% of the kids qualified for free or reduced lunch. While there was certainly violence and drug use in my neighborhood, my parents protected me as much as they could. Once I started working as an engineer, I saw the harmful ways people viewed people like my family members. One assumption I commonly saw is that poor people do not have financial literacy, which causes them to make bad choices. The reality is that poor people are usually choosing the least bad choice from a list of bad choices.

Disabled. I consider myself disabled because of my autism, depression, and chronic pain. On the outside I look able-bodied, which means people are not seeing any device or prosthetic helping me get through the world. When I worked in corporate America, I struggled with explaining the accommodations I needed to feel productive. After describing the chronic pain and associated depression I was experiencing at work, one boss said one word: "Wow." In my year end review, he gave me the lowest performance rating possible.

Bisexual. I was a late bloomer and explored my sexuality after college. Bisexuality is an identity associated with privilege, because I am often assumed to be straight when I am with my male partners. In sex-positive communities such as BDSM, polyamory, and swinging, bisexual women are highly sought after because they are perceived to be available to both men and women for group sex. My sexuality was what led me to the progressive communities that I am a part of today. The deeper I went into sex-positive lifestyles, the more out of place I felt with my home culture. At the same time, I saw that the people who worked so diligently on promoting radical living were clueless to the reality that marginalized people lived. That's how I found my niche.

I have had crises about some aspects of my identity and readily accepted others. At this point in my life, I'm OK with all of them. Some people in your community may struggle with

> You may have various feelings or opinions about race, sexuality, and gender identity, but spare me and your Tokens. If you want diversity, you need to be open to identities that are foreign or even repulsive to you. If you've bought this book to argue with me about that, I appreciate the donation.

their identity. You may see them one way while they identify a different way. It's not your job to classify people. Let them self-identity, and do your best to support them.

Now that you've read about the basics of identity, set up a discussion with your community members about their identity and privilege. Suggested discussion questions and resources are included below.

WORK BOOK) Identity and Privilege

Length: One Hour
Format: Small Groups
Tokens Present: No
Resources (see Tools and Resources): Social Identity Wheel, Diversity Profile, My Multiple Social Positions.

Introduction

Explain to participants that you are going to discuss identity. Identity refers not just to how we perceive ourselves, but how others see us. Do not allow white participants to get out of acknowledging their whiteness by pointing to their ancestors.

Even if someone identifies as a certain ethnicity, the broad category of whiteness is associated with privilege. We as human beings process information quickly, and that means we see people as either white or non-white when we first meet them. Give your members time to process that discrepancy.

Discussion Questions

1. Describe how you identify and what feelings come up around each category.
2. What identities have you thought about often? What identities are more in the background for you?
3. What are some ways that the way people see you differ from the way you see yourself?
4. Are there any identities that you feel pride around?
5. Which of your identities are associated with privilege, and where have you seen that privilege in effect?
6. Do you have any feelings of shame or guilt around identifying as part of a privileged group?
7. What are some good aspects of having privilege?
8. How aware are you of the difficulties less privileged people face? Have you ever thought of them as less motivated, less resourceful, or less skilled at navigating life?
9. What groups are in the majority in your community? Do you see places where the community is more comfortable for those people than others?
10. Think about the people in your network of friends and colleagues. How are they similar to you? Do you find that you have fewer close friends who are less privileged?
11. Have you ever told someone that you are color-blind or that you don't see their difference?
12. What types of people would you like to see more of in your community?

Implicit Bias:
Life as a Mega Stuf™ Oreo©

I studied in Russia for six weeks during college. My parents and instructors worried about my safety because I was the only Black student, but the truth was that everyday reactions to my race were more hurtful than the violent hooligans I was warned about. My very first day in St. Petersburg, two white women stood beside me to take photos without asking me. This happened multiple times. I got so used to the game that I started asking them to take one with my camera. One man grabbed me for a picture and summed it up in one word: "A statue!" I was a curiosity, a monument to the diversity of Russia. No one ever asked me about my life and my goals because that wasn't important. To them, I was just a prop.

My awareness of my identity is always in relation to the people around me. When I'm out in public, I'm aware that I'm Black and female. When I'm at home, the only thing I'm aware of is that I like Mega Stuf™ Oreos© a little too much. When you meet people, you project a lifetime's worth of vocabulary, lifestyle, and history onto them. That's called implicit bias. Very few people, no matter how "woke," are able to avoid these mental shortcuts and deal with people based on their individual presentation.

When you rely on implicit bias, the marginalized person has to live with the gap in between your assumption and reality. We are the ones who have to convince you of our usefulness. I was diagnosed autistic at age 33. By that time, I had received two college degrees, held multiple jobs, bought a house, married a person, divorced that person, sold the house, raised a child, and otherwise meaningfully participated in society. I am capable, and I shouldn't have to tell you any of that for you to believe me. When I point out that implicit bias caused you to think less of me, you tell me that you didn't mean to underestimate me. But the truth is, you did mean to. It's not my bias. It's yours.

We can't speak for all experiences, but marginalized people can give a perspective on our particular difficulties. We know how to navigate a world that is not built for us. The more time you spend listening to your Tokens, the more you will see them as humans just like you.

Implicit bias is an innocent act, but it causes real harm. When discussing implicit bias with your community members, don't gloss over the fact that your marginalized community

Oreo is a derogatory term for Black people who don't appear to fit into Black culture. They are "white on the inside." When I was in school, I was told I acted white because I spoke standard (not proper) English, placed in advanced classes, and had white friends. It took me years to understand my mental block around being friends with and dating Black people. Bias is not just something people in the majority have. It exists in marginalized communities as well. When it comes to implicit bias, there is work to do for everyone.

members may need to heal from harm caused by your privileged members. Ignore the temptation to help your privileged members feel better by offering an apology and a promise to do better. Hold them accountable while giving your less privileged members space to express their pain.

WORK BOOK) Implicit Bias

Length: One to Two Hours
Format: Large Group
Tokens Present: Yes
Resources (see Tools and Resources): "White Privilege: Unpacking the Invisible Knapsack" by Peggy McIntosh, privilege walk.

Use this session as an opportunity for privileged members to listen to less privileged ones. Focus on one or maximum two aspects of identity to keep the conversation productive. Give your Tokens the choice to attend and talk about ways they have experienced bias and microaggressions. This is not the time for members to self-identify as part of a less privileged group. If a member stands up to talk about their previously undisclosed marginalized identity (such as being mixed race, queer, or disabled), ask them to save their story for the next discussion. When hearing the Tokens' stories, privileged participants will inevitably want to talk about their feelings of guilt or shame. Do not let these voices dominate the conversation. After the discussion, ask your privileged members to give the Tokens space and wait at least a day before reaching out to them to talk about what they shared. Emphasize that they should ask for consent before diving into a discussion about their identity.

Introduction

Discuss implicit bias and how everyone has bias whether we are conscious of it or not. Cover the ways bias influences our actions, and how it shows up in the larger community. Discuss common stereotypes and assumptions you make about different types of people. Then explain that you are going to spend this time listening to the voices of the people with less privilege. These people have been previously identified and asked to share their stories. If a member is not among them and wants to speak, invite them to share in small groups during the next exercise.

Questions for Tokens

1. What are some assumptions people have made about you? Were they accurate or inaccurate?
2. What are some ways that people have used their assumptions against you?
3. What parts of your life have been harder due to your lack of privilege?
4. What are some ways you change your behavior to avoid bias?
5. What has been your experience of being the Other, in this community and others?
6. What are your thoughts about being part of this particular community? Have you felt welcomed or uncomfortable?
7. What would you like your community members to know about being less privileged?

After the Tokens have had time to speak, continue to the next exercise with your privileged members only. Encourage the Tokens to meet separately to provide support to one another. When you place one or two Tokens in majority privileged groups after a discussion like this, it may turn into an interrogation about their experiences instead of forcing the privileged members to process their feelings.

Microaggressions,
or, It's Just a Compliment!

I was at a sex-positive retreat when a new acquaintance asked about my hair. I had been wearing my hair short and natural (just long enough to be nappy) for years. I told the group at my table how Black people often grow up dissatisfied with their hair. Many of us have used chemical straighteners for all or part of our lives. Embracing my natural hair was similar to embracing my sexuality—it was a personal journey, and I came out more enlightened and willing to educate others. My acquaintance was white and wanted to touch my hair. Before I go further, please remember:

Never Touch Someone's Hair.

I'm not even limiting this to Black people because it's just common sense. Many "ethnic" people have had the experience of someone wanting to see if our hair was real or comment on how beautiful it was. My body is not here for your viewing and tactile pleasure. I'm not fishing for compliments; I'm trying to survive as a Token.

I let the acquaintance touch my hair, but I told them later that it felt harmful because it was a microaggression. A microaggression is an unintentionally harmful act toward or statement about a marginalized person. If you're white, you've probably been accused of committing a microaggression before. If you haven't, keep reading. Microaggressions are often the opposite of aggression: sometimes they are meant as compliments. The problem is they usually set the person apart as a Token instead of part of the community.

Your people are hard workers.

Your hair is so pretty!

Do I call you "she" or "he?"

How do you say your name again? Does your family live in America?

You have a cool accent. I love eating soul food.

Your hair is so pretty!

You are so articulate. Did you go to school here?

Does your family live in America? **You speak English well.**

You are an inspiration.

Did you grow up in a bad neighborhood?

I walked into an [ethnicity] restaurant once and I felt so out of place.

Where are you from? Really?

You're not like other [marginalized] people.

Do you have a lot of brothers and sisters?

I don't see you as [marginalized identity].

I'm sorry I used the wrong gender. I'm still getting used to it.

I've been to [foreign country] before.

I've heard [your ethnicity] is really friendly to foreigners.

I know how to say "Hello" in [foreign language].

Once I had training at a machine shop led by older white men. One instructor had a great time teasing me for being a woman and not knowing how to use the tools, but I was used to that. I was not prepared when his buddy talked about having Black coworkers at his plant. "You people are all right," he said approvingly.

Microaggressive phrases are not bad out of context, and marginalized people understand that you're trying to connect. Comments like these are often followed up with personal questions about our language, family, or education. Here's the thing: we didn't invite you to start talking about our identity. One person's curiosity is fine. Multiple people's curiosity over time is exhausting. When a Token only talks to people about how they are different, they start to feel unwelcome, and they may not come back. Encourage your community members to think before they speak. If you're interacting with someone and your first thought is to comment on something related to their race, gender, or language, stop. You're about to commit a microaggression.

Imagine you are back in high school, and your archenemy has bad acne that makes her self-conscious. One day you decide to needle her and you say, "Your makeup looks great today!" If you can give a back-handed compliment, you know what a microaggression feels like. You can't pretend you were just being nice if you are already aware of the social and personal implications of a statement (and from now on, you are aware of those implications.)

There's a thin line to walk with Tokens. On one hand, you don't want to erase someone's identity by saying, "I didn't even notice you were X." On the other, you don't want to make harmful assumptions about them based on what you think you know. For me, it's enough to say, "I recognize that you are Black, and I know that means you may have had a different life than

I have. Can I ask you about that?" A respectful question gives them the choice to share or not. Don't be offended if they've filled their quota of curiosity for the day and they say no.

Microaggressions hurt, but we rarely tell you when they do. The reason we don't tell you is because it'll hurt your feelings. When it comes to race, that's called white fragility. It's not because you, as a white person, are too insecure to talk about race. It's because you can't engage on a topic like race without feeling defensive. White fragility turns harmful events into pity parties. When a person of color suggests that a white person acted out of ignorance or prejudice, the white person hears, "You are a bad person."

Understandably, their nervous system goes into overdrive trying to fix that perception. The conversation may devolve into passionate speeches, tearful explanations, or, worse, trying to extract an apology from the other person. This is not helpful. This is why you can't just tell your Tokens, "Let us know if anything happens." When something happens, the person involved may get so upset that it's not worth the Token's emotional energy.

Marginalized people point out microaggressions because they want to help people who are close to them. When a Token tells you that your words are a microaggression, they're keying you in to a part of their world you've so far been unaware of. They want you to know that you may have meant it a certain way, but it didn't come out that way. The appropriate way to respond to someone pointing out a microaggression is to say, "Thank you." That's it. It's OK to feel bad that you have hurt people. It's OK to feel upset that no one has ever told you. It's not OK to break out into tears because you feel bad. We already feel bad. For you.

Use the following discussion guide to help your privileged members talk about the ways they may have harmed less privileged members. Give them time and space away from your Tokens to process the feelings of indignation, guilt, or shame. This is an important part of The Work, but it should not be done at the expense of your Tokens' mental well-being.

WORK BOOK Microaggressions

Length: One to Two Hours
Format: Small Groups
Tokens Present: No
Resources (see Tools and Resources): Examples of Racial Microaggressions, "Racial Microaggressions in Everyday Life" by Derald Wing Sue.

Discussion Questions

1. When talking about bias and microaggressions, what was hard for you to hear?
2. What are ways you have tried to connect to people who have a difference?
3. What have your interactions with marginalized people been like? Do you see them in a variety of situations, or only as service workers, students, or some other disadvantaged group?
4. Did you see yourself committing some of the micro-aggressions described?
5. If you have feelings of guilt or shame around a particular incident, do you feel a need to make it right or apologize? Do you think they need to hear an apology from you, or is it just to make you feel better?
6. Has someone ever called you out on a microaggression? What was your response? What would you do differently?

7. Can you think of opportunities in your life to speak up about bias and microaggressions?
8. What are some aspects of your identity where you have experienced bias or microaggressions?
9. Do you see yourself as part of the majority group in this community? Are there ways that you have felt like a Token?
10. How will you talk to your friends and family about your learnings?

Majority Culture:
What's Yours Is Mine

When I talk about microaggressions, I'm talking about things that are OK to do in majority culture. In North America and Western Europe, majority culture is middle-class white culture. I've heard white people say that they don't have a culture, but they do. White culture is expecting a junior person to call a senior person sir or ma'am. White culture is politely agreeing with someone and fuming about it later. White culture is asking where the bathroom is when you can see the door down the hall just fine. Do these examples sound mundane? That's because they are. White culture is set up as the standard.

My first time experiencing white culture was at church. In my city, Black people were historically excluded from the white mainstream churches. In middle and high school, I attended a residential summer program that offered to drive us to church on Sundays. One of the options for church was Baptist, so I chose that one. That's when I learned there is a difference between white and Black Baptists. White Baptists sang. Black Baptists danced, shouted, and ran down the aisles. White Baptists gave a sermon. Black Baptists preached. White Baptists sat for an hour and went out to eat at the local restaurant. Black Baptists usually didn't leave until the football game started.

The white church was a different and not unpleasant experience, but it taught me that I had to be flexible when dealing with different cultures. I am not going to shout at a white Baptist church just because it was what I grew up with. When I'm in a place with a different majority culture, I have to fit in or I will be pushed out. The marginalized people in your community have learned to be flexible just like I have. It's called code-switching, and it can be tiring. If your community as a whole was able to flex around different cultures, more people would share the load, and, as a result, we could all bring more of ourselves to the events.

Don't adopt practices of a minority culture in order to "fix" majority culture. Not only does it result in stares from your mainstream parents, it harms the creators of that culture. Minorities do not have the opportunity to pick and choose what they enjoy of their identity. Black people, for instance, can not be Black when they're cooking and white when they're up for promotion. Culture is formed out of a shared sense of history and, at times, struggle. Trying on the practices of a minority culture like accessories reinforces oppression because it says, "I see things you are good at. It's mine now."

This is particularly a problem with white progressive communities, which have taken on the practices of many minority cultures: yoga, cacao ceremonies, and drumming as examples. All of these practices were initially seen as backward or primitive, only to be elevated as spiritual and intuitive once a privileged person started doing it. You may absolve yourself by saying you—or, at least, someone you know—learned from a teacher who is respected in that culture, but that doesn't mean you can freely use it. Even minorities have their price, and you should pay it if you intend on continuing the practice. Giving money to a minority practitioner won't make you less of an oppressor, but it will put food on the table. Either way, do some soul-searching and defer to the people you think you are honoring when using their practices.

The final step of examining majority culture is sharing your learning with others. If you have privilege, then you have a responsibility to help other privileged people understand that marginalized people are marginalized because of your culture. This is when you need to unblock people on social media and start engaging them in conversation. Help them understand that the key to diversity is not ignoring differences, but celebrating them. Teach them what you've been learning about bias, microaggressions, and privilege. Don't lecture and don't insult them. If they want to know more, they will ask. If they vehemently disagree, be the better person. Focus on maintaining the relationship so that they know who to turn to when they have questions. Know that they, like you, started in a place where they had no Black friends to tell them these things.

I understand that many people feel like the other side is actively harming them with negative social media posts or that their anxiety about current events leaves them with no energy to engage. This is the only time I would invite you to compare your suffering to marginalized people who experience

I was a debutante in a ball sponsored by a Black sorority. We learned how to set a dinner table, do our makeup, and dance like high society girls. There's a belief among some Black people that assimilation is the way to elevate the Black community. If we learn how to tie a tie and give a firm handshake, we will eventually be equal to white people. I won a scholarship from that sorority, but they ran out of funds before I went to college. It's not proper manners that makes people equal.

difficulties in real life. Don't avoid conflict just because it's hard. If you don't talk to the other side, you're abdicating your responsibility to speak the truth and enact real change. We, the marginalized people, are already sacrificing our well-being to work with you. Oppression is something that people can grow out of. Consider if you too have things to grow out of.

WORK BOOK Majority Culture

Length: 30–45 Minutes
Format: Large Group
Tokens Present: No
Resources (see Tools and Resources): Acts & Omissions, "White Supremacy Culture" by Tema Okun.

Use this session to discuss cultural norms in your community. Explain that "majority culture" is the set of norms associated with being white and middle-class. If your community's majority is different, explain what the majority culture is before starting the discussion.

Discussion Questions

1. What aspects of majority culture do you see in your community?
2. What are some ways your community is different from majority culture?
3. What are some ways that your community's culture differs from your home culture (the culture you grew up in)?
4. Did you join the community in part to get away from majority culture? Is it what you hoped?

5. What type of orientation do members receive when coming into your community?

6. What are some ways you've had difficulty adjusting to the community's culture?

7. What are some faux pas people have committed in the community? How did members respond?

8. What conflicts have you had with members that you attribute to their culture?

9. What are some good parts of your community's culture?

10. What are problematic parts of your community's culture? How is your culture exclusive or unwelcoming?

11. Have you ever found yourself apologizing for your community's culture? What prompted the apology and how was it received?

12. Has anyone ever spoken about changing part of your community's culture? What was the collective response?

13. What ways have you challenged your home culture with friends or family?

14. What are some suggestions for leaders to help change the community's culture to be more inclusive?

Have a separate discussion with your Tokens to get their feedback about the community. Keep in mind that some of them may have specific instances of harm to talk about. Place the experiences in the context of the larger community and commit to making systemic change. Follow up with individual members after the discussion to ask what specific steps would help correct the wrongs.

Discussion for Tokens With Leadership

1. What ways have you felt welcome or unwelcome in the community?

2. What culture clashes have you experienced?
3. What suggestions would you make about changing the community's culture?
4. What pushback have you seen in trying to address cultural differences?
5. How can the leadership be supportive of you as a minority member?

Creating Culture Conscious Meetings

Imagine you're in a hotel, and you're looking for your community's conference room. When you open the door on bikers sitting in front of a skull and crossbones, are you with your people? What if it's elderly white ladies knitting? As the Tokens, your minority members are used to feeling out of place every time they come in. The good news is that you can make some changes so that your events or workplace feel more inclusive. These changes won't guarantee that marginalized people will be lining up to join, but it might be enough to get them in the door.

Know that there is a small slice of Tokens that are comfortable being in majority spaces, either because of their upbringing or by conscious choice. They may not think of their marginalizations until someone brings it up. They are often told they are "one of the good ones" because they don't conform to stereotypes. They may not strongly identify with their identity's culture, but that doesn't mean they don't value it. These unflappable Tokens are not the ones you are trying to bring to your events. They will show up regardless because they want to participate in community. You are trying to reach those who see that your community is full of privileged people and think, "This is not the place for me."

I was very nervous the first time I went to a gay church. The Metropolitan Community Church was a typical church building with a rainbow flag out front. There were mostly middle-class white people, but I saw other Black people too. They all smiled at me, but *they didn't turn on the Red Alert for New People. The usher hand-ing out name tags asked if I wanted a hug, and I was happy to re-ceive one. I found a seat in the back, and no one rushed over to chat me up. After the sermon, someone invited me to the fellowship hall for lunch. I sat with people who asked where I was from and what I was doing in the city. They didn't ask me to self-identify, and they didn't change anything about the way they operated because I was there. It was a naturally inclusive place.*

The Invitation

First, consider how and where you are advertising your group. Many communities advertise meetings on social media or in public spaces. When you go to post your flier, check out the people in the room. Are the clientele mostly white and middle-class? Is there a place down the street that might have more young and queer people? Are there more Black Lives Matter signs than Black people? People have to see your message to respond to it. While you may consider your favorite spots to be diverse, the reality is that they often are not. If you are looking for a specific category of people, seek out the places where those people choose to be.

Be realistic about who you are reaching on social media. If you make a post and ask people to share it, the people who see it are very likely to have similar interests and networks to your own. Unless you have done The Work to cultivate friendships with different types of people (your Black neighbor doesn't count), your reach will be limited to people like you.

Appearance is an important part of an invitation as well. If you search for a stock photo of a family, that family is very likely to be white and heterosexual. Have you ever looked at the front cover of *Essence* magazine? The people on the cover are almost always Black, because that's who they want to read their magazines. Has that ever stopped a white person from reading it? Never. Treat your advertising copy the same way.

When you make an invitation, you might be used to using words like "Ladies and gentlemen" or "men and women." The world has changed, and many people identify as nonbinary or gender nonconforming. That means you might be excluding people who don't feel comfortable with the traditional categories. Is it vital to your mission that you call people out by gender? If not, try to be inclusive. Say people, folks, pirates, or something else to signal that you are not enforcing a gender binary.

Many adults have children, and some are single parents. If your community is geared toward families, offer childcare when you can. Parents are less able to participate in community when they can't afford childcare or don't have generous family members nearby. If your events are kid-friendly, say so. Work with parents to create a space that allows for children who will occasionally cry, fight, and run.

When my daughter was a toddler, I started attending Al-Anon meetings. Not only was I the youngest woman there, I was the only one with a child. None of the meetings offered childcare. My toddler was fussy and busy, but the women in the group were gracious. When we were guests at a different meeting, the leader was not so kind. "She doesn't need to be here," the leader said in my direction. Imagine if I had missed out on healing because I was shamed for bringing my kid.

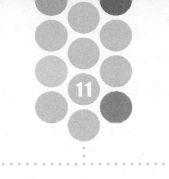

The Location

One of my favorite tools is the Racial Dot Map. This map shows the United States population as a series of dots. The dots are colored to represent the racial category each person chose on the census. Take a moment to look up your neighborhood on the map. Is there a whole bunch of blue where you are? Are there streets that show a clear divide between Black and white, or white and Asian? These dots show the legacy of housing segregation. If you think you're exempt because your city is liberal or not in the South, you're wrong.

The reality is that there are white and Black neighborhoods, and, in bigger cities, there are neighborhoods for other minorities too. There are very specific ways the government and homeowners have made minorities feel unwelcome in certain areas. That means that people who don't fit in will be, at best, looked over suspiciously, and, at worst, have the police called on them. It doesn't matter if you personally have never seen this happen. Minorities have a cultural memory, and many will be hesitant about showing up in majority white neighborhoods.

I once dated a white man who lived in the suburbs. He invited me and my daughter to his house to swim in the neighborhood pool. My daughter loves swimming, so we were excited to get to the gate early, along with several other white families.

When the pool attendant opened the gate, the white families gave their house number and went on their way. My partner gave his, but the attendant looked at me and my daughter.

"Where are they from?" she asked.
"They're with me," my partner said.
"Do you have ID?" she asked. "We charge $2 for guests."

My partner was confused, but I knew exactly what was happening. I was a Black woman in a white space, and I wasn't welcome. I was furious. The attendant was young, so I couldn't blame it on old age or ignorance. I knew that she had grown up with a natural suspicion of minorities in majority white spaces. My partner floundered and tried to find cash, but the attendant eventually let us in "this time." Later my partner asked his teenage son about the guest fee, and he said they never enforced it with him.

When your gathering place is in a white neighborhood, minorities may not feel welcome. The occasional presence of one or two people of color does not change that. Think about what your location says when planning your community meetings. Is it a white church in a wealthy neighborhood? Is it the college grad hangout? Is it the community center in the hood? "But I know the people who own the building and they're great," you may say. That just tells me you know how to network with people who look like you. Is it so difficult to go a street over and start a relationship with a minority business owner?

Am I telling you that if you set your event in a minority neighborhood, more minorities will come? Yes, but it's complicated. Minority neighborhoods on average have higher crime rates. Due to higher mortgage interest rates and lower home equity, buildings may be older and less maintained. That's not something this book or your Work can change. If your community members are worried about crime, they may not come out no matter what race they are. If it's a safe place (and you can determine this by talking to the owners, not by making assumptions), then minorities may still see that your event is majority white and decide they're just not interested. They may (correctly) think that you are pandering to them and wonder if you have actually done The Work to be an inclusive organization. The only way you can fight that perception is to consistently show up in that community and contribute to it as a member, not a benefactor.

If your location is anywhere in the rural backcountry, good luck.

Accessibility is important for community members with disabilities. Does the building have wheelchair ramps that are easy to get to? Is the location too loud for hard of hearing folks to stay engaged? Does the place burn incense that may keep people with sensory sensitivities away? You may say, "None of that bothers me or my friends." If you are able-bodied, you don't understand how certain environments may be unsuitable. The good news is that you can make your location more accessible, and those changes are best made with the input of people with the type of disability you're accommodating. Don't guess at a fix and expect people to come flooding in.

Is your location accessible by public transportation? There are plenty of people that can't afford a car and would appreciate a ride. If you're expecting everyone to use ride sharing, remember that many low-income people don't have a checking account to link to the app even if they own a smartphone. Is it a restaurant where everyone is expected to buy dinner? It can be humiliating to attend and not eat, especially when people ask why or offer to pay for their food. Will your members who don't drink or are in recovery look out of place if they don't have a beer at the table? Is your favorite spot the one full of tobacco and vape smoke?

If you're considering an outdoor location, what are the facilities like? I know earlier I said Black people like to camp, but there's a reason we don't have a big presence at Burning Man. Those of us near rural areas have a cultural memory of sundown towns and threats against the out of place traveler. There's also the tendency for white progressives to relish in "roughing it" with no running water or heat, when low-income families are "living it" without the benefit of organic groceries.

Introductions

The actual act of welcoming people can be inclusive or exclusionary. Do you sit in a circle or facing a lectern? Do you have space for wheelchair users or is everyone expected to squeeze through tight spaces? On the other hand, asking everyone to sit on the floor may mean the person with arthritis isn't going to come back. Forcing all the newcomers to sit up front may extract any energy your introverts had for making friends.

Do you insist on hugging everyone who walks in the door? Do you ask for their name and then make a joke when it is foreign sounding or hard to pronounce? Do you try to pay extra special attention to the minority who just walked in and is still sizing up the place? All of these are ways that you can put people off from attending your event. Yes, it's true: some people don't like hugs.

The language you use when introducing people is important as well. Common practice in progressive communities is to invite people to say their name and their pronouns. For example, "I'm Crystal, and my pronouns are she/her/hers." I don't recommend doing this right away if it is not common practice in your group. If you insist on announcing pronouns during introductions, your gender nonconforming members may feel like they are being put on the spot. Your community may also react negatively to asking for pronouns. They may say, "I don't care what you call me," or "I'm obviously a he." Make sure your community has done The Work around gender so they don't harm people. Invite people to give their pronouns in a one-on-one setting if you are wondering about their gender identity. Once your community feels comfortable giving their pronouns one-on-one, implement the practice of introducing your pronouns with your name.

If you are going to start your meeting with any type of cultural action, please run it by several leaders and Tokens. I don't care if your friend from a reservation taught you the song. Is it appropriate for the space, is it part of your heritage, and is it used with permission? White culture has just as many songs and traditions that you can borrow from without being problematic.

I was out of town at a conference where an uncomfortable number of people were waving at me as if they knew me. Finally one woman walked up very excited to show me her tattoo that said Namaste. Finally I understood: they were confusing me for another Black woman who had spoken earlier. Her name was Namaste. (Black people can also be guilty of cultural appropriation!) One unfortunate consequence of being a Token is getting confused with other Tokens. These situations are always ironic to me because I could honestly be mistaken for someone else—my twin sister, a scholar who attends a completely different set of conferences. Misidentifying someone is embarrassing, and the only way to avoid it is to train your members to recognize people for things other than their skin and hair. Make it a practice to wear name tags or do icebreakers where people talk about a unique trait or favorite activity. If you do trip up, own up to it quickly without self-flagellation.

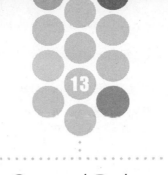

Ground Rules

Create a culture of respect for every meeting by establishing ground rules. For example, encourage people to listen to each other instead of waiting to respond. Back someone up if their story is being challenged for authenticity. Don't allow insults or demeaning comments. Make agreements on confidentiality outside of the group. Have a clear process for resolving disputes.

Be conscious of how dress codes can be discriminatory. Face control, a policy practiced in Russia and other former Soviet countries, excludes people based on dress from nightclubs and restaurants. If your location has rules against bandanas, saggy pants, headscarves, or sneakers, minorities will feel less welcome. It's not that Black men don't have belts: they are expressing themselves through their style. If you're ballroom dancing, dress codes make sense. If it's only to make white people feel comfortable, they don't.

If your community has anything to do with sex, sexuality, swinging, BDSM, polyamory, or other types of "lifestyles," set up very specific ground rules at your meetings and events. People often join these groups expecting to find partners for "fun" (sex), and they will assume the environment is more open than traditional spaces. Whether that is true or not, be clear on how people should interact with each other.

If you want people to feel safe, establish protocols about how to ask for a date or "to play." Some groups have a rule that you must meet in person before reaching out online through social media. Some groups require people to be "vetted," or approved by other members, before they attend more intimate events. Do not expect people to follow rules that you have not announced or posted clearly. Have the leadership actively monitor people and step in when someone looks uncomfortable. Follow up immediately on any claims of assault or harassment.

Minority women are often fetishized at events. I attended a sexual play party once, and during the nonsexual beginning activities, women were invited to stand up and close their eyes. The men circled the room and whispered their thoughts to whomever they cared to. By the time I heard, "You are exactly what I've been looking for," my skin was crawling. Don't ignore the potential for boundary violations at your sex positive events. What may seem like a compliment to you could make another person feel unsafe.

Conversation and Conflict

Vary your meeting styles to attract different people to different events. Some people enjoy free-flowing conversation, while others need structured prompts to be able to participate. Some people like to be active and moving, while others come to sit and relax. Be aware of how culture affects conversation style. In some Black families, loud debates and derisive comments are a form of connection. Acting that way in a majority white space may lead to members saying they feel threatened or otherwise uncomfortable.

In my experience as an autistic person, conversation can be a minefield. I answer questions directly, and I don't always understand nuance. I am at the point in my awareness where I can warn people that I am this way, but other neurodivergent people may not know why they have difficulty in social situations. Explore the topic in a discussion or in your diversity training. This is the only time I would make an exception to the Token rule: many autistic people love to talk about themselves and what their world is like. Ask them if they feel comfortable leading a discussion about their differences for the community and ask what accommodations will make them feel supported when they do.

If you decide to limit devices at your meetings, consider allowing exceptions for people who use them to communicate or self-soothe. Just because you find them distracting and mindless doesn't mean others do. These people should not be confronted and asked to defend their use to leadership or other members. As long as the policy has been clearly communicated, trust that they are able to use them without disturbing other members or breaking the perceived peace of the space.

Conflict is an inevitable part of any group process. As a leader, the way you handle conflict will tell the rest of the group how to behave. Do you squash vocal opposition, prompting people to talk behind your back? Do you encourage shouting matches as long as people hug it out afterward? Create guidelines for how your community deals with disagreements. Teach people to debate ideas, not personalities. Avoid protecting people with more social capital. Seek to understand the underlying conflicts instead of just dealing with surface issues.

Nonviolent communication (NVC) has been taken up by a lot of progressive groups for its structure and clarity in expressing feelings. Many people who grew up avoiding conflict have found their voice through NVC. There are, however, power differentials that can make NVC ineffective. If either party is less educated or less practiced in NVC, they will have a disadvantage during a conflict. If someone refuses to engage unless the proper NVC format and/or words are used, they may be abusing the process to get their desired outcome instead of letting both parties express themselves. Instead of defaulting to NVC, think about whether community members need other ways to navigate conflict.

Many progressive communities deal with problematic people by "cancelling" or excluding them from the community. This method may work on Twitter, but if you treat all your members this way, you'll burn through the member rolls. Many of us Tokens are used to sitting through conversations that are blatantly racist, sexist, or otherwise harmful. We don't point it out because (1) we too desire social inclusion, (2) we don't know who will back us up, or (3) we don't have the energy for an argument. Instead of shaming, use your privilege to help others understand harm. When the problem is simply using the wrong words or making an off-color joke, address the issue in private. You in turn can practice being vulnerable with people who are trying to do their best. If you are in an environment where you constantly feel unsafe, you may be more primed for external triggers. Reconsider being in a community that allows that kind of harm.

Another dynamic that happens to Black women is being invalidated when they are emotional or angry. Showing emotion means we immediately lose any argument that's supposed to be rational and fact-based. Everyone has bad days, but Black women are expected to be a sassy, upbeat sidekick all the time. Once I had a difficult conversation with a boss, I was on the verge of tears from anger. I asked to be excused. Later my boss told me that I couldn't handle criticism. Ironically, the people I had chosen to be around for their lack of drama left me without the space I needed to take care of my emotions.

Saying Good-bye and Feedback

Some people like to slip out the door when an event ends. Some people like to linger and talk. Does your space allow for both? Will the meeting facilitator be busy cleaning up, or do they have time for questions? Make at least one leader available after meetings to address private questions or concerns. You can make a statement to that effect and have your contact information readily available. Some people will come up right away, while others may need to think about their request and follow up with an email or phone call.

The first time I visited the church across from my new house, two ladies showed up shortly after service with some baked goods. In my old neighborhood, the only unexpected visitors we got were the police and proselytizers. Know how your actions may be perceived by someone from a different culture. People into BDSM, for example, may not want public contact with the group leader. Same for queer people who may not be out to their family. Think before you approach a new friend in public or in the virtual world. People may have alternate profiles on social media and want to compartmentalize their hobbies. Posting on someone's wall or inviting them to an event may out them before they are ready to have that conversation.

The Workbook:
Making Community-Wide Change

Now that your community has done some of The Work and understands ways to be culture conscious, brainstorm ways to make changes. Start by accepting all ideas without criticism or discussions about feasibility. Members may be tempted to argue against a particular idea because it doesn't sit well with them or their expectations. Their arguments may discourage others from contributing ideas, so minimize these types of interruptions during brainstorming.

Once all the ideas are listed and adequately described, have your leadership discuss the ones that feel the most urgent and/or significant. Come to an agreement about the overall ideas instead of discussing specifics about implementation or expected outcomes. Acknowledge that some ideas are radical and may cause division, but don't avoid change just because it is hard. Your community may be ready for the challenge.

If your ideas revolve around economic justice, avoid thinking that people are less because they have less. For instance, if you are making some of your homes in your cohousing community affordable, don't assume that the people who live in those homes are incompatible with your culture. Think about the assumptions you are making about those people and ways that you can welcome them into a flexible and comfortable community.

Narrow down the list of ideas to five to ten using a process such as dot voting or consensus. Present the narrowed-down list to your members and discuss the intentions and expected consequences. Now is the time to allow members to voice opposition or support. Facilitate the conversation so that specific Tokens or leaders are not attacked. Present the ideas as a united front instead of one person's agenda. Use a voting tool to narrow down the ideas to one to three ideas to implement in the next six months. Ask for volunteers to form a task force to work with leadership on moving the ideas forward. Do not force Tokens to participate on the task force, even if one of the ideas is theirs. Give them the choice to opt in or out of the process instead of holding the expectation that they will lead the change.

After a few months, hold a discussion about the proposed ideas and get feedback on the changes people see. If possible, get feedback from your Tokens separately so they can be candid and honest about what is working and what is not. If they have experienced personal attacks, commit to addressing those while still moving forward. If the majority of the community is extremely resistant and negative toward the process, engage a facilitator to help navigate the conflict and change course if necessary. This is The Work, and while it may be hard, it should not damage the community beyond repair.

Avoid the temptation to talk about your implemented idea as a success story to other communities. There are no one-size-fits-all approaches, and if you are only a few years into a change, you may not be aware of the actual challenges. The Tokens that have benefited from that change may not be completely happy with the situation. Instead of gratitude, they may feel—well, like Tokens. If you are going to share best practices, get feedback from your Tokens and ask how they would represent the process to an outsider. Invite them to speak about it instead of relying on your privileged members. Focus on the effect the change has had on marginalized members instead of the good feelings the privileged members have from implementing it.

Length: 30–45 Minutes
Format: Large Group
Tokens Present: No

1. What changes have been implemented in the community?
2. What was hard about making those changes?
3. What positive and negative ways has your community changed?
4. Think about the original list of ideas. Was your community being realistic?
5. Should you keep working from that list or develop new ideas?
6. What conflicts came up around the specific changes? How were they handled?
7. Did you lose community members? How well did you handle their departure?
8. In what ways did your leadership and community members grow?
9. What do your Tokens think about the changes? What are their priorities going forward?
10. Did you gain new members as a result of the changes?
11. What learnings would you like to share with other communities? Who should represent your community in sharing that knowledge?

Limits to Inclusion—
It's Not About You Until It Is

A Space for Us

Even when you implement changes in your community, marginalized people will choose to make their own spaces. We create these spaces because we need time to be in our own culture with no exceptions. In these spaces, we share our triumphs and struggles with people who understand. We find peace and healing, wisdom and love. If you are not one of us, these spaces are not for you.

If your organization has a critical mass of people with a shared identity, ask if that group wants space for them at your events or in separate meetings. Offer to schedule and pay for time at your main venue or another space for this purpose. Even if the leadership creates this space, give your Tokens the power to design the programming and aesthetics to suit themselves.

You may ask, "But isn't that reverse discrimination?" No. Discrimination is an act of disempowerment by privileged people. Minority-only spaces are a way of taking back power. It's a healing space, and it doesn't mean the world is going to become more segregated. If you're still frustrated that minorities need their own spaces, examine why you think you can control access to any space. Why is your opinion about access more important than a minority organizer's? Privileged people are used to getting their way, and it feels wrong to be told "no." Feel into that discomfort when you think about creating exclusive spaces.

How Not to Recruit Leaders

There are benefits to having Tokens in your leadership. People who have the skills to navigate multiple cultures are valuable. They can point out areas where the organization is failing and give credibility to your efforts to be more inclusive. But don't reach out to any marginalized person just because they fit in a specific category. If you only see them as representing their area of marginalization, you may not see them as full people with strengths and weaknesses of their own. It is fine to call for leadership from a certain category, but make sure you have done The Work to avoid bias and microaggressions. Many marginalized people get into leadership only to be told that they are too forceful or disruptive. If you don't make cultural space for marginalized leaders, you are using them as Tokens.

A few years ago, I spoke about diversity at a conference. Shortly after the conference, the sponsoring organization invited me to apply to be on the board. I looked at the application process and compared my resume to the other board members. They were professionals and leaders, and many of them had been involved in the community for decades. I had been involved in the community for two years. I was a local organizer, but that conference was the first time I'd met many of movers and shakers at a national level. I made the only logical conclusion: They wanted me because I was Black. Being on the board meant regular volunteer work and self-funded travel to retreats and conferences. At the time, I was working as a substitute teacher and freelancer. I literally couldn't afford to volunteer. I sent a polite email to the chair explaining how women and minorities are often asked to do a disproportionate amount of unpaid labor, and that I was unwilling to work without compensation.

If you see someone doing important work, it's fine to approach them and tell them they're doing a good job. If you're going to invite them to participate in your community, consider paying them. If you feel resistance to paying them when a privileged person would do it for free, think about what in our history has led to people, especially white women, having abundant free time. Often those women had minority women cooking for them, cleaning their homes, and raising their children. Middle-class white women benefit from the wealth of their ancestors in being able to afford childcare and transportation while working, whereas many Black, Hispanic, and lower-income women rely on subsidized childcare and school buses.

When you think about people who might be a good fit for your organization, think beyond your network. You may believe that you evaluate each person you meet fairly based on their merits, but research has shown that we like people who look like us. That means you're probably not recommending your Token friend for every job opportunity. If it is, you're probably congratulating yourself on your open-mindedness instead of wondering why you only know one qualified minority. Marginalized people understand that dynamic, and we look out for each other. That's why Hispanic directors hire Hispanic writers, Black legislators hire Black staffers, and why your town has so many Chinese restaurants. We like to be with people who look like us, but we also have to work against white people's tendency to only network with other white people. You may ask, "But shouldn't we dream of a world where everyone is judged by the content of their character?" Dream away. And, for the time being, overcorrect so that marginalized people can get to the point of being judged solely on their merits.

Keep On Keepin' On

The Work is hard, and the results are not guaranteed. I hope that you remember the difference you are making for your marginalized members while you are in the midst of making changes. If one more person feels included and accepted in your community, that is one more person that can help fulfill your mission and vision. If it causes two or three or more people to leave, so be it. They can fulfill a different vision that is less inclusive. They can live in a world where differences don't matter and people are expected to shut up and fit in. Somewhere like Portland, Oregon.

Last year, I went to Portland for a conference. I'm not one to prejudge (I'm more likely to post-judge) so I kept an open mind when I went to explore the neighborhood around our meeting space. I walked down the street—five or six blocks during a busy lunch hour, and I didn't see a single Black person. Not among the store patrons, not among the bus drivers, and not even among the homeless.

There's a particular type of loneliness you feel when you are the Token. It's not the loneliness of having no friends, because we can usually find people with similar interests. It's not the same as missing family, because God knows we leave them for a reason. It's a loneliness of culture, where the people around me don't know what it's like to get your hair wet or don't have a preference between orange or purple soda. To be in a place with no one like me means I'm not a member of the community. I'm just a visitor, and I always will be.

This is not the time to tell me about your trip to Africa where you felt different because you were white. It doesn't compare to living in a world where you are ignored, underestimated, and discriminated against on a regular basis. It's hard. I'm telling you it's hard, and you don't have to come up with a response other than, "I hear you. And I'm going to do better."

Tools and Resources

Books

The Work

DiAngelo, Robin. *White Fragility: Why it's So Hard for White People to Talk About Race*. Boston: Beacon Press, 2018.

Fleming, Crystal Marie. *How to Be Less Stupid About Race: On Racism, White Supremacy, and the Racial Divide*. Boston: Beacon Press, 2018.

Kendi, Ibram X. *How to Be an Antiracist*. NY: One World, 2019.

Kivel, Paul. *Uprooting Racism: How White People Can Work for Racial Justice*, 4th ed. Gabriola Island: New Society, 2017.

Oluo, Ijeoma. *So You Want to Talk About Race*. Seattle: Seal Press, 2018.

Saad, Layla F. *Me and White Supremacy: Combat Racism, Change the World, and Become a Good Ancestor*. Naperville IL: Sourcebooks, 2020.

Sue, Derald Wing. *Race Talk and the Conspiracy of Silence: Understanding and Facilitating Difficult Dialogues on Race*. Hoboken NJ: Wiley, 2016.

Sullivan, Shannon. *Good White People: The Problem with Middle-Class White Anti-Racism*. Albany NY: State University of New York Press, 2014.

Tochluk, Shelly. *Witnessing Whiteness: The Need to Talk About Race and How to Do It*, 2nd ed. Philadelphia PA: R&L Education, 2010.

Biography

Coates, Ta-Nehisi. *Between the World and Me*. NY: Spiegel & Grau, 2015.

Irving, Debby. *Waking Up White, and Finding Myself in the Story of Race*. Elephant Room Press, 2014.

Menakem, Resmaa. *My Grandmother's Hands: Racialized Trauma and the Pathway to Mending Our Hearts and Bodies*. Las Vegas NV: Central Recovery Press, 2017.

Segrest, Mab. *Memoir of a Race Traitor: Fighting Racism in the American South*. New York: New Press, 2019.

Stevenson, Bryan. *Just Mercy: A Story of Justice and Redemption*. NY: Spiegel & Grau, 2015.

Thompson, Becky. *A Promise and a Way of Life: White Antiracist Activism*. Minneapolis: University of Minnesota, 2001.

History of Race

Alexander, Michelle. *The New Jim Crow: Mass Incarceration in the Age of Colorblindness*. NY: New Press, 2010.

Battalora, Jacqueline. *Birth of a White Nation: The Invention of White People and Its Relevance Today*. Houston TX: Strategic Book Publishing, 2013.

DeGruy, Joy. *Post Traumatic Slave Syndrome*, rev. and updated ed. Joy DeGruy Publishing, 2017. joydegruy.com/shop.

Kendi, Ibram X. *Stamped From the Beginning: The Definitive History of Racist Ideas in America*. NY: Bold Type/Hachette, 2017.

Painter, Nell Irvin. *The History of White People*. NY: Norton, 2010.

Roberts, Dorothy. *Fatal Invention : How Science, Politics, and Big Business Re-create Race in the Twenty-First Century*. NY: New Press, 2011.

Rothstein, Richard. *The Color of Law: A Forgotten History of How Our Government Segregated America*. NY: Liveright, 2018.

Tatum, Beverly Daniel. *Why Are All the Black Kids Sitting Together in the Cafeteria? And Other Conversations About Race*, rev. and updated ed. NY: Basic Books, 2017.

Wise, Tim. *Colorblind: The Rise of Post-Racial Politics and the Retreat from Racial Equity*. San Francisco: City Lights, 2010.

Commentary

Baldwin, James. *The Fire Next Time*. NY: Vintage, 1992.

Coates, Ta-Nehisi. *We Were Eight Years In Power: An American Tragedy*. NY: One World, 2018.

Du Bois, W. E. B. *The Souls of Black Folk*. Mineola NY: Dover, 2014. First published 1903 by A.C. McClurg (Chicago).

Dyson, Michael Eric. *Tears We Cannot Stop: A Sermon to White America*. NY: St. Martin's Press, 2017.

Documentaries and Podcasts

Biewen, John. Seeing White. 14-part podcast, February–August, 2017. Scene on Radio. sceneonradio.org/seeing-white/

California Newsreel. 2003. *RACE: The Power of an Illusion*. Three-part documentary film. racepowerofanillusion.org/

Duvernay, Ava, dir. *13th*. Kandoo Films, 2016, 100 min.

Internet Resources

The Work

"Acts & Omissions," *Building a Multi-Ethnic, Inclusive & Antiracist Organization: Tools for Liberation Packet*, Safehouse Progressive Alliance for Nonviolence, 2005, p. 5, racialequitytools.org/resource files/olcese.pdf

AWARE-LA. White Anti-Racist Culture Building Toolkit. awarela.org /toolkit

Challenging White Supremacy Workshop. cwsworkshop.org /resources.html

"Diversity Profile," Stockton University, A Booklet of Interactive Exercises to Explore Our Differences, 2011, Exercise #2, p. 7, intraweb.stockton.edu/eyos/affirmative_action/content/docs /Interactive%20Diversity%20Booklet%2010-14-2011%20Rev %203_1_16.pdf

dRworks. Dismantling Racism Workbook. dismantlingracism.org

"Examples of Racial Microaggressions." University of Minnesota, School of Public Health. sph.umn.edu/site/docs/hewg/micro aggressions.pdf

Goldbach, Jeremy. "Activity Five: Class and Historical Disadvantage." The MSW@USC Diversity Toolkit: A Guide to Discussing Identity, Power and Privilege, May 7, 2019. msw.usc.edu/mswusc-blog /diversity-workshop-guide-to-discussing-identity-power-and -privilege/#cross

Greenberg, Jon. Curriculum for White Americans to Educate Themselves on Race and Racism—from Ferguson to Charleston. Citizenship & Social Justice, July 10, 2015. citizenshipandsocialjustice.com /2015/07/10/curriculum-for-white-americans-to-educate-them selves-on-race-and-racism/

McIntosh, Peggy, "White Privilege: Unpacking the Invisible Knapsack," *Independent School*, Winter 1990, racialequitytools.org/resource files/mcintosh.pdf

"My Multiple Social Positions," Handout 5.1 from *Witnessing Whiteness*. witnessingwhiteness.com/wp-content/uploads/2014/06 /handout5-1multiple_social_positions.pdf

Okun, Tema. "White Supremacy Culture." Dismantling Racism Workbook. dismantlingracism.org/uploads/4/3/5/7/43579015/whitesup cul13.pdf

"Opportunities for White People in the Fight for Racial Justice," whiteaccomplices.org

"privilege walk [complete]," edge.psu.edu/workshops/mc/power /privilegewalk.shtml in "Introduction to Power and Privilege." Penn State University, 2006. edge.psu.edu/workshops/mc/power

"Project Implicit," implicit.harvard.edu/implicit

"Sample Activities & Templates for Exploring Privilege, Power, and Oppression." University of Michigan Inclusive Teaching. sites.lsa .umich.edu/inclusive-teaching/sample-activities-templates/

"Social Identity Wheel." Adapted by the Program on Intergroup Relations and the Spectrum Center, University of Michigan. August 16, 2017. sites.lsa.umich.edu/inclusive-teaching/2017/08/16/social -identity-wheel/

Sue, Derald Wing. "Racial Microaggressions in Everyday Life," *Psychology Today*, October 5, 2010, psychologytoday.com/ca/blog/micro aggressions-in-everyday-life/201010/racial-microaggressions-in -everyday-life

Teaching Tolerance. tolerance.org

History

Mapping Inequality: Redlining in New Deal America. dsl.richmond.edu /panorama/redlining

The Racial Dot Map: One Dot Per Person for the Entire United States. Demographics Research Group, Weldon Cooper Center for Public Service, University of Virginia, July 2013. demographics.virginia .edu/DotMap

The 1619 Project. nytimes.com/interactive/2019/08/14/magazine /1619-america-slavery.html

Commentary

Hackman, Rose. 2015. "'We need co-conspirators, not allies': how white Americans can fight racism." *The Guardian*, June 25, 2015. theguardian.com/world/2015/jun/26/how-white-americans-can -fight-racism

Hutcherson, Lori Lakin. 2017. "My White Friend Asked Me on Face-book to Explain White Privilege. I Decided to Be Honest." *YES! Magazine*, September 8, 2017. yesmagazine.org/people-power/my -white-friend-asked-me-on-facebook-to-explain-white-privilege -i-decided-to-be-honest-20170809

Lemieux, Jamilah. "Weinstein, White Tears, and the Boundaries of Black Women's Empathy." *Cassius*, November 2, 2017. cassiuslife .com/33564/white-women-dont-look-out-for-black-victims/

Phipps, Alison. "The Political Whiteness of #MeToo." *genders, bodies, politics*. June 4, 2019. genderate.wordpress.com/2019/06/04 /metoo/

Turner, Dwight. 2018. "'You Shall Not Replace Us!' White suprem-acy, psychotherapy, and decolonisation." *British Journal of Med-ical Psychology* 18, no.1 (March). researchgate.net/publication /324890681_'You_Shall_Not_Replace_Us'_White_supremacy _psychotherapy_and_decolonisation

Organizations

AORTA—Anti-Oppression Resource and Training Alliance. aorta.coop

Class Action: Building Bridges Across the Class Divide. classism.org

Organizing Against Racism. oaralliance.org/

Racial Equity Tools. racialequitytools.org/home

Showing Up for Racial Justice. showingupforracialjustice.org/about .html

Whites for Racial Equity. whitesforracialequity.org

Index

About the Author

CRYSTAL BYRD FARMER is an engineer turned educator. She has been an organizer and speaker as part of the cohousing and polyamorous communities. She is the website editor for Black & Poly, an organization promoting healthy polyamorous relationships for Black people. She also serves on the  Editorial Review Board of *Communities* magazine published by the Global Ecovillage Network-United States. She is passionate about encouraging people to change their perspectives on diversity, relationships, and the world. Crystal lives in Gastonia, North Carolina.

Find out more about Crystal and her work at: bigsisterteams.com/diversity.

More Resources from
New Society Publishers

Powerful strategies and practical tools for white people committed to racial justice
Uprooting Racism—4th Edition
How White People Can Work for Racial Justice
Paul Kivel
6 × 9" / 448 pages
US/Can $24.99
ISBN 9780865718654

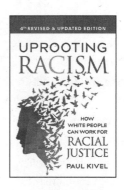

Building environmental strength through a diversity of youth
Engage, Connect, Protect
Empowering Diverse Youth as Environmental Leaders
Angelou Ezeilo
6 × 9" / 240 pages
US/Can $19.99
ISBN 9780865719187

Redefining the face of the American farmer
The Color of Food
Stories of Race, Resilience and Farming
Natasha Bowens
8 × 9" / 240 pages / full color
US/Can $29.95
ISBN 9780865717893

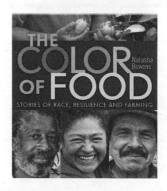

ABOUT NEW SOCIETY PUBLISHERS

New Society Publishers is an activist, solutions-oriented publisher focused on publishing books for a world of change. Our books offer tips, tools, and insights from leading experts in sustainable building, homesteading, climate change, environment, conscientious commerce, renewable energy, and more—positive solutions for troubled times.

We're proud to hold to the highest environmental and social standards of any publisher in North America. When you buy New Society books, you are part of the solution!

DON'T EAT THIS BOOK *(but you could)*

- We print all our books in North America, never overseas
- All our books are printed on **100% post-consumer recycled paper**, processed chlorine-free, with low-VOC vegetable-based inks (since 2002)
- Our corporate structure is an innovative employee shareholder agreement, so we're one-third employee-owned (since 2015)
- We're carbon-neutral (since 2006)
- We're certified as a B Corporation (since 2016)

At New Society Publishers, we care deeply about *what* we publish—but also about *how* we do business.

Download our catalog at https://newsociety.com/Our-Catalog or for a printed copy please email info@newsocietypub.com or call 1-800-567-6772 ext 111.

ENVIRONMENTAL BENEFITS STATEMENT

New Society Publishers saved the following resources by printing the pages of this book on chlorine free paper made with 100% post-consumer waste.

TREES	WATER	ENERGY	SOLID WASTE	GREENHOUSE GASES
13	**1,100**	**6**	**45**	**5,700**
FULLY GROWN	GALLONS	MILLION BTUs	POUNDS	POUNDS

Environmental impact estimates were made using the Environmental Paper Network Paper Calculator 4.0. For more information visit www.papercalculator.org.

Certified **B** Corporation

MIX
Paper from responsible sources
FSC www.fsc.org **FSC® C016245**

new society
PUBLISHERS
www.newsociety.com